I VOW

Fifty-Two Poetic Promises for a Meaningful Life

VANELLI

For every heart that has known both sorrow and joy,
these vows are for you.

Acknowledgments

To my family and friends, thank you for inspiring these pages. Your hours of listening, those long talks, and your presence during heavy moments helped these poems find their way. You've been the breath behind every line.

To my cousin Nick, you walk through life with a quiet strength and stoic grace. Watching you, I understand why you were Dad's favorite. You remind me that calm isn't weakness, it's power in stillness.

To Mike Kubeisy, brother, thank you for always being just a phone call away. You don't sugarcoat, you don't dance around the truth, you deliver it straight with love. Your honesty keeps me anchored, and your loyalty has been a gift I never take for granted.

To my Skylum teammates, thank you for creating, supporting, and remaining hopeful, even in wartime. Your quiet strength reminds the world what it means to endure with heart.

To Amber, your transformation from rock bottom to lifting others is nothing short of remarkable. Your resilience, your courage, and your heart for others inspire me endlessly. You are living proof that healing is possible and that purpose grows from pain.

To the strangers who became storytellers, whether we met in passing, online, or through shared vulnerability, thank you for trusting me with your pain, your hope, and your truth. Your stories gave this book its pulse.

To you, the reader, thank you for opening *I Vow*. Whether you came looking for something or just stumbled upon it, I hope you find yourself in these words and leave feeling seen.

And to God the Father, thank You for entrusting a deeply flawed man with a message of love, intention, and neighborly grace. None of this is mine, it's Yours, and I'm just trying to pass it on.

With all my heart,

–Vanell

Contents

To the One Holding This Book

Each vow in this book was written in a quiet moment of truth. Some came from pain, others from clarity. All are promises we can make to ourselves: to live with intention, kindness, and strength.

This collection is not about perfection. It is about presence. About finding stillness in the noise, courage in uncertainty, and meaning in the ordinary. These are not just words on a page. They are quiet companions, reminders that we shape our lives one small vow at a time.

These vows came together slowly. Many were sparked by conversations with friends, family, and even strangers. People opened up about what they were carrying. Sometimes they just needed someone to listen. I paid attention to what was said, and what wasn't. In those moments, I didn't feel the need to offer advice. I felt called to write a vow. A small, honest promise that could hold the weight of what they were feeling.

Other times, the inspiration came from within. In the moments I wasn't proud of how I showed up, I took time to reflect, how did I act, and how did I want to act next time? From that space came another vow. Not one of perfection, but of intention.

This book is for anyone in that same space. Anyone rebuilding, carrying grief, regret, exhaustion, or questions they don't yet have answers to. It is for those who rise each day without feeling ready, who carry on quietly, and keep trying even when strength feels far away.

There is no right way to read these pages. You can move through them one vow per week, or flip to what calls to you. Let the words meet you where you are. They are not here to fix you. They are here to walk beside you.

If you take one thing from these pages, let it be this: you do not have to be ready to change everything. Just be willing to make one quiet, honest promise to yourself and keep it.

That is where everything begins.

– Vanelli

•

Today I will

choose truth,
even if my voice
trembles. I will
stand in who
I am, act with
purpose, and
refuse to let
fear decide my
direction.

• • •

The Fire That Begins The Walk

COURAGE & CONVICTION

There comes a time when silence becomes too heavy to carry, when staying small costs more than being seen. These are the moments that test our spine, when fear presses close, and yet something within us refuses to back down. That something is courage. And it does not roar, it rises.

Conviction is not about always being right. It's about standing in what you know to be true, even when uncomfortable. Even when it costs you. It's the choice to keep showing up with integrity, to let your actions reflect your values, and to hold steady when the world tries to pull you off course.

The poems in this chapter are forged in moments of pressure, when the stakes were high, the risks were real, and the temptation to disappear was strong. They honor those who have spoken through shaking voices, taken steps with unsure feet, and stood their ground not because it was easy, but because it mattered.

These vows are declarations of presence. Of strength that doesn't always feel like strength, and bravery that lives alongside fear, not in the absence of it. They are reminders that your voice has power, your choices shape the world around you, and your life is worth showing up for.

I Vow Not to Remain Silent

I vow to stop pretending calm,
when silence brings the greatest harm.
No peace is true if built on fear,
or paid by swallowing what's clear.

I will not shrink or blur my tone,
to ease the weight I do not own.
I'll speak with care, but not erase
the truths that time will not replace.

I will stay kind, but won't recede,
when silence serves another's need.
Not every storm is mine to stall,
some reckonings must rise and call.

I will choose calm when it brings light,
but not mistake it for what's right.
I'll ask myself, "Is peace what's true,
or just a role I'm slipping to?"

So when the silence strains my chest,
and truth no longer stays at rest,
I'll break the hush and call what's meant,
I vow not to remain silent.

•

Today I will

honor my voice
and speak the
truth, even when
it is difficult,
choosing
authenticity over
comfort.

. . .

I Vow to Speak with Courage

I vow to meet the world full-faced,
To speak with courage, firm and laced.
My words will burn but never harm,
A steady flame, not force or charm.

I will not flinch when truth feels hard,
Or yield my voice to drop my guard.
In silence loud, in crowded fight,
I will be centered, clear, and right.

I will choose love, though edged with steel,
Let kindness shape the strength I feel.
I will not hide when wrong is loud,
But lift what's true, and stand unbowed.

I will not bend to fear or blame,
But move like one who's walked through flame.
I'll be the ground when feet can't stay,
A compass voice to guide the way.

So when the moment asks of me
To lead with fire and dignity,
I'll hold my place, unmoved, alone,
I vow to speak with courage, and stand like stone.

•

Today I will

speak with
fearless clarity,
stay grounded
in truth, and
allow kindness
to define the
strength I bring
into the world.

• • •

I Vow to Honor My Voice

I vow to speak, even when it's hard,
To trust my words and drop my guard.
They may not come out smooth or right,
But I won't dim to make them light.

I will not wait for perfect calm,
Or shrink my thoughts to keep the balm.
I'll think things through, then speak them plain,
What matters most is I remain.

I won't compete to be the loudest,
Or make my truth sound more well-rounded.
Even when doubt is in the room,
I'll say what's mine, not just assume.

I'll be respectful, not withdrawn,
And choose what's real to carry on.
When I feel small or out of place,
I'll stay right here, I'll hold my space.

So when the world distorts my sound,
And shakes the place where I am found,
I'll stay with what I know by choice,
And vow to honor my own voice

Today I will

trust my
voice, even in
discomfort, and
hold space for
my truth with
courage.

•   •   •

I Vow to Always Be Free for Me

I vow to stand where I feel right,
Not where I'm told to dim my light.
No playing small, no false agree,
I choose what feels like home to me.

I will stop trying to please the room,
Or hold my breath to shift their mood.
When silence asks too much of me,
I'll speak, and still stay kind and free.

I will walk paths that match my pace,
Not chase approval, praise, or place.
I won't pretend to fit some mold,
My life is mine, not bought or sold.

I will check in before I act,
Make sure I'm not just losing track.
What works for others might not fit,
And I'll be fine just knowing it.

So when the world pulls loud and tight,
I won't give up my quiet right.
I'll answer only honestly,
For I vow to always be free for me.

•

Today I will

honor my truth
over conformity
and choose the
freedom to be
fully myself.

• • •

I Vow to Defend What Matters

I vow to stand where truth is thin,
To name what's right and let it in.
I'll trust the pull I feel inside,
And not let fear decide I hide.

I will defend the unheard voice,
Not just in words, but in my choice.
I'll hold the line when none appear,
And stay behind when others clear.

I will defend what justice needs,
In quiet acts and daily deeds.
Not just with signs or shouted names,
But in the way I play the game.

I will defend what I believe,
Even when others twist and leave.
I'll live it real, not just recite,
And walk it through the hardest night.

So when the weight is mine to bear,
And right and wrong hang in the air,
I'll plant my feet against the chatter,
Shouting my vow to defend what matters.

Today I will

I will honor my
principles not
only in words
but in how I act
when it counts
most.

• • •

I Vow to Act with Integrity

I vow to choose the honest way,
Even when silence might let me stay.
To hold my ground when others cease,
And answer pressure with quiet peace.

I will speak truth though it might cost,
Refuse the game when trust is lost.
I won't reshape myself to fit,
Or trade my name for shallow grit.

I will pause when the moment sways,
Notice the weight of what I say.
I'll clear my lens when judgment blurs,
And own the space my choice confers.

I will stand in the light I claim,
Even when shadows call my name.
I'll mend what's mine, both loud and small,
And let my actions speak it all.

So when the mirror shows my face,
I'll meet my eyes and hold my place.
I'll stand in truth and quietly be,
For I vow to act with integrity.

Today I will

align my choices
with my values,
even when no
one is watching.

. . .

I Vow to Stay True When It's Tough

I vow to meet myself where I stand,
Not only when life goes as planned.
When things fall apart or pressure is high,
I won't pretend or live a lie.

I will say what's true, even if small,
Even if no one hears it at all.
I'll stay with tension when it appears,
And face what's real instead of fears.

I will pause when I don't feel sure,
And trust in what I choose to endure.
Not every moment needs to be loud,
Sometimes quiet makes me proud.

I will walk through doubt with steady breath,
And not mistake hard days for death.
The path gets made by how I move,
Not by how much I have to prove.

So when I feel pushed to fake or bend,
I'll hold my shape and not pretend.
Even unseen, I'll say I'm enough,
I vow to stay true when it's tough.

Today I will

honor my truth
even when it's
difficult, knowing
that strength lies
in authenticity.

. . .

I Vow to Live with Strength and Honor

I vow to hold my name with care,
To meet each dawn in humble prayer.
In storm or stillness, loss or fight,
I choose the path that honors light.

I will not let pride lead my way,
But walk with honesty each day.
When anger stirs or shadows grow,
I'll pause to breathe before I show.

I will protect what must endure,
My word kept clean, my motives pure.
I'll do what's right when none can see,
And hold that truth with loyalty.

I will not seek the crowd's acclaim,
But root my worth in inner flame.
I'll shape my strength through daily grace,
And hold to purpose in my place.

So when the world grows loud and wide,
I'll hold my ground with measured stride.
I craft a life that will not stray,
I vow to live with strength and honor every day.

•

Today I will

stay rooted in my
principles, act
with deliberate
grace, and define
my worth not
by external
validation, but
by the strength
of my own
convictions.

• • •

I Vow to Stand Tall and Find the Sunshine

I vow to meet the day with lifted eyes,
To seek out warmth where sorrow lies.
Even as endings shift the ground,
I'll listen for the softer sound.

I will not shrink when love lets go,
Or fear the space where hurt will grow.
I'll breathe in deep, unclench my hands,
And trust the ground on which I stand.

I will return to what feels true,
Fresh air, kind words, the morning dew.
A quiet walk, a friend nearby,
Will bring me back when fears run high.

I will not wait for peace to land,
I'll shape it gently with my hand.
A window's light, a page, a song,
These daily roots will keep me strong.

So when the storm leans into view,
I'll meet it whole and pushing through.
My roots will ground, my eyes will shine,
I vow to stand tall and find the sunshine.

●

Today I will

plant myself
firmly in the
truth of who I
am, find strength
in the small and
sacred, and shape
peace with my
own hands, even
when the skies
turn gray.

• • •

•

Today I will

let go of what no
longer helps me
heal. I will speak
to myself with
compassion and
make space for
softness where
shame once
existed.

• • •

What the Wound Taught Me

HEALING & FORGIVENESS

Healing doesn't always arrive with a breakthrough or a dramatic release. More often, it's the quiet, steady work of tending to what's been broken. It's the moment you meet your reflection with softness instead of shame. When you stop replaying what you should've done and begin honoring what you've survived.

Forgiveness is often misunderstood. It's not about forgetting or excusing what hurt you. It's about choosing not to let pain shape your identity. It's the decision to set down what was never yours to carry. Not because it wasn't heavy, but because you're ready to live unburdened. Forgiveness isn't weakness. It's an inner strength.

These poems sit beside sorrow without rushing it. They give space to wounds that still sting and memories that never quite faded. They hold space for the stories that didn't end the way we wanted, the apologies we never received, and the guilt we're learning to let go. They aren't about rewriting the past but loosening its hold.

The vows here offer something quieter than perfection: compassion. A promise to stand by your healing without judgment. To be patient with what's still mending. To make peace with who you were while giving grace to who you're becoming. This isn't about fixing. It's about accepting. And in that acceptance, I found my way back to wholeness.

I Vow to Acknowledge My Story

I vow to honor all I've lived,
Each jagged edge, each gift life gives.
My past holds weight, but not regret,
It's where my soul and truth have met.

I will not hide what shaped my days,
But offer it in honest praise.
In sharing pain, I open doors
For others drifting from their shores.

I will remember where I broke,
The prayers I whispered, barely spoke.
And testify to grace that came,
A quiet hand, a steady flame.

I will not wait for perfect time,
Or craft each word into a rhyme.
If just one heart begins to see,
Then truth has done its work through me.

So when the past begins to press,
I'll meet the weight with gentleness.
I'll live my truth with steady glory,
For I vow to acknowledge my story.

Today I will

honor my
journey, share
my truth openly,
and trust that my
story can help
someone else find
their way.

. . .

I Vow to Stop Carrying Blame

I vow to stop the silent game,
Of holding on to hidden shame.
What wasn't mine, I set it down;
I won't mistake the bruise for crown.

I will not scan each room for wrong,
Then twist myself to just belong.
I'll name what hurt, but not take blame
For fires I didn't set to flame.

I will release the need to bend,
To patch what others won't defend.
When silence falls, I'll let it land,
Not rush to prove or understand.

I will find peace in honest ground,
Where past regrets don't chase me down.
I'll own what's mine, no more, no less,
And let false guilt grow quiet, rest.

So when the urge to shrink appears,
I'll meet it with a voice that clears,
And live unburdened by old shame,
I vow to stop carrying blame.

•

Today I will

release the
weight of blame
that isn't mine
and reclaim peace
through truth
and
self-compassion.

• • •

I Vow Not to Hunger for Their Validation

I vow to name the ache I've known,
The quiet pull when I'm alone,
To see the ways I chase the light,
And ask the world to make me right.

I will not chase a shifting crowd,
Or shape my words to make them proud.
I'll speak with care, but not to please,
And leave my soul unclenched, at ease.

I will remind myself each day,
That praise will pass, then slip away,
And when it fades, I will not sink,
I'm rooted deeper than they think.

I will find peace in work well done,
Not seeking praise from anyone.
No mirror's tilt, no lifted brow,
Can shape the truth I carry now.

So when the silence wraps around,
I'll stand in stillness, safe and sound,
No longer needing their affirmation,
I vow not to hunger for their validation.

•

Today I will

trust my own
voice and value,
letting go of
the need for
validation from
others.

• • •

I Vow Not to Live in Jealousy

I vow to free my guarded heart,
To let comparison depart.
No life but mine is mine to tend,
No race to chase, no soul to bend.

I will not measure side by side,
Or fold my worth to fit their stride.
Instead, I'll plant with steady care,
A soul that roots in its own air.

I will recall what's meant for me,
Can't be shaken, can't break free.
In every turn, in every fall,
I'll trust the rhythm holding all.

I will meet envy with soft eyes,
And listen past its brittle cries.
A gentler voice will clear my view,
To bless what's real, and hold what's true.

So when I feel the ache ignite,
I'll calm it with a clearer sight.
I'll lift my soul that longs to be,
For I vow not to live in jealousy.

·

Today I will

focus on my
unique journey
and celebrate
others without
diminishing my
own light.

• • •

I Vow to Cut My Ties With Desperation

I vow to stop the frantic chase,
That leaves me strained and out of place.
The grasping hands, the urgent plea,
No longer take the heart from me.

I will not beg what will not stay,
And fold myself to clear the way.
I'll listen close and stand up tall,
And meet the hush without a wall.

I will find ground beneath my feet,
And breathe in rhythms slow, discreet.
When silence comes, I won't defend,
I'll let it teach, I'll let it mend.

I will not measure worth by lack,
Or chase what's always turning back.
With open palms and steady grace,
I'll meet each moment face to face.

So when the hunger pulls me near,
To grasp for what won't reappear,
I'll gently choose a calmer station,
I vow to cut my ties with desperation.

Today I will

release my need
to cling, and
trust that what
is meant for me
will meet me in
peace.

. . .

I Vow to Let Go of Doubt and Fear

I vow to stop the rush to hide,
To meet my fear with arms open wide.
No longer ruled by anxious pace,
I choose to stand and take my place.

I will speak gently when I shake,
And name the thoughts that make me break.
I won't pretend I feel no doubt,
But I will walk the longer route.

I will move forward, slow but true,
Without the proof I once clung to.
Each act of faith, however small,
Will be the step that says I call.

I will breathe deep and plant my feet,
In present ground where calm and strength meet.
I'll trade the urge to disappear
For words that say, "I still am here."

So when the weight begins to press,
I'll rise with quiet steadiness.
This is the life I choose to steer,
I vow to let go of doubt and fear.

Today I will

honor my fears
without letting
them define
me. I will take
deliberate steps
toward the life I
choose, knowing
that courage is
built in each
small act of
presence and
persistence.

• • •

I Vow to Never Regret My Past

I vow to honor where I've been,
The quiet loss, the buried win.
Each step, each scar, each winding way
Has shaped the soul I hold today.

I will not flinch when old scenes rise,
Or trade their truth for softer lies.
I'll let the pain be fully known,
A page that helped me stand alone.

I will not carry what has been
As weight that pulls me back again.
I'll take what's useful, leave what's worn,
And greet each day as though reborn.

I will forgive what I outgrew,
And name the fires that once felt true.
I'll speak of then without disguise,
A thread, not something to revise.

So when the past begins to speak,
I'll listen close but will not seek.
Its voice may stir, but not outlast.
I vow to never regret my past.

●

Today I will

honor my past as
a teacher, not a
prison, carrying
forward only
what strengthens
my spirit.

• • •

I Vow to Be Patient with Myself

I vow to meet the rush with rest,
To loosen what I once called best.
To trade the climb for grounded still,
And trust in progress shaped by will.

I will not chase another's pace,
But walk in step with quiet grace.
I'll let each lesson shape my core,
Not grasp for less or hunger for more.

I will respond with steady breath,
Not fold beneath imaginary death.
When plans dissolve, I will remain,
And sift the gift beneath the strain.

I will make space for all I feel,
And meet my truths the way they heal.
The path is slow, the learning deep,
And peace is something I will keep.

So when I stray or lose my way,
I'll honor what the pauses say.
Each breath, a truth I hold in stealth,
I vow to be patient with myself.

Today I will

give myself the
grace of patience
and allow every
moment to
unfold with
mindful care.

• • •

I Vow to Give Even When I'm Empty

I vow to meet the weight you bear,
Though I have little strength to spare.
My arms are tired, my hands move slow,
But still, I let my giving show.

I will not wait to feel restored
Before I open up what's stored.
Whatever light I have to lend,
I'll pass along and not pretend.

I will not hide behind my ache,
Or let my silence start to break.
The words I speak to carry through
Will steady me while holding you.

I will let care reshape my pace,
And meet each need with quiet grace.
Not out of strength or perfect health,
But from a deeper kind of wealth.

So when I feel my edges thin,
And wonder what remains within,
I'll draw from love that lives in me,
I vow to give even when I'm empty.

•

Today I will

give what I can,
knowing that
love shared from
an imperfect
place carries
profound power.

• • •

•

Today I will

pause. I will
breathe. I
will meet this
moment with
openness, and
choose to be
fully here, as I
am.

. . .

The Sacred Now

PRESENCE & AWARENESS

The world moves fast, so fast that we often miss our own lives in the blur, rushing through days, reacting without pause, reaching for the next thing before we've even had a chance to feel the last. Yet beneath the noise, something quieter waits: a steady stillness, a guiding voice, a deeper sense of being that doesn't demand more from us but gently asks that we simply arrive, fully present, here and now.

These vows are an invitation to return, to yourself, to the present moment, to the life unfolding in real time. They ask us to slow down and pay attention, not because the world demands it but because we need it. To be present is to choose awareness over autopilot, attention over distraction, meaning over motion.

The poems in this chapter hold space for breath, for stillness, for silence. They honor the sacredness of small things: a sip of warm tea, the softness of morning light, the feeling of your own feet on solid ground. These are not moments to race past. They are moments that remind us we are alive.

Presence is not about perfection. It is about noticing. Awareness is not about control. It is about compassion. The vows here are gentle yet firm. They call us to listen more deeply, to rest more intentionally, and to live each moment with care. This is not just mindfulness; it's a form of reverence.

I Vow to Focus on What I Can Control

I vow to meet the day as it arrives,
To leave behind what fear supplies.
The wind may change, the tide may turn,
But I'll take in what I can learn.

I will not chase the shifting sky
Or waste my strength on asking why.
I'll keep my eyes on what is near
And guard the space I hold most dear.

I will release what isn't mine,
The clock, the crowd, the crooked line.
Instead, I'll shape what's in my care,
The breath I take, the way I share.

I will not yield to creeping doubt
Or need to sort the chaos out.
Each twist of fate is not my role;
I plant my roots to keep me whole.

So when the storm begins to grow
And pulls me where I shouldn't go,
I'll breathe, return to what is whole,
I vow to focus on what I can control.

•

Today I will

center myself on
actions within
my reach and
trust the process
unfolding around
me.

• • •

I Vow Not to Judge Anyone

I vow to quiet thoughts that chase
The urge to place, define, or erase.
We don't know what another hides,
Or all they carry deep inside.

I will not name a soul unkind
For what I glimpse and leave behind.
A sigh, a scowl, a hurried tone,
May rise from battles fought alone.

I will remind myself to stay
With open hands throughout the day.
A stranger's anger, cold or heat,
May trace back to a small defeat.

I'll think of Him who wore a crown of thorn,
Who came to heal the bruised and worn.
He walked beside the lost and shamed,
Not to condemn, but to love us the same.

So I will meet the world with grace,
Look softer at each passing face.
Each life's a war not always won,
I vow not to judge anyone.

Today I will

pause before
passing
judgment,
remembering
that every soul is
fighting battles
I cannot see.
I will choose
understanding
over reaction,
and compassion
over critique.

. . .

I Vow to Move at My Own Pace

I vow to move at my own pace,
To trust my rhythm, not the race.
The world may spin, the clocks may call,
But I won't rush to catch it all.

I will not chase the crowded sound,
Or seek applause from those around.
I'll listen where the quiet grows,
And plant my steps in what I know.

I will protect the time I need,
To shape my thoughts before they lead.
I'll breathe beneath the weight of day,
And find my steadiness that way.

I will remember slowness heals,
That truth is felt, not forced or sealed.
The bloom is not more true for speed,
Or every moment born to lead.

So, when the world begins to roar,
I'll ground myself in something more,
A quiet strength, a rooted grace.
I vow to move at my own pace.

Today I will

honor my
natural rhythm
and create space
for peace to guide
my way.

•   •   •

I Vow to Make Myself a Priority

I vow to make myself a place,
Where quiet breath can move with grace.
No more the last to feel the light,
No longer dimmed to keep things right.

I will not wait to break apart,
Before I tend to my beating heart.
I'll honor where my needs begin,
And claim the strength I hold within.

I will not flinch when I am still,
Or chase the praise that bends my will.
I'll choose the calm, the slower pace,
And offer presence over race.

I will not stretch beyond what's true,
And shape myself to fit a view.
I'll mark the edges I define,
And trust the voice I know is mine.

So when the world distorts my name,
And pulls me far from where I came,
I'll turn within, not try to flee,
I vow to make myself a priority.

•

Today I will

put myself first
with compassion,
choosing to
nurture my well-
being without
guilt and letting
my inner voice
lead the way.

• • •

I Vow to Show Up as Myself

I vow to meet each day I wake,
with nothing hidden, nothing fake.
Though pressure calls me to perform,
I'll walk beyond the scripted norm.

I will not fold to fit the frame
that dims my voice or shifts my name.
I'll speak with calm, without disguise,
and meet the world with steady eyes.

I will not twist to please the crowd
or chase approval wrapped in loud.
Instead, I'll listen, breathe, and stay,
where truth and quiet light the way.

I will wear joy without retreat
and let my sorrow find its seat.
With kindness firm, I'll mark the line
between what's yours and what is mine.

So when I'm tested, cracked, or thrown,
I will not vanish from my own.
I'll rise, unarmored, not in stealth,
For I vow to show up as myself.

•

Today I will

embrace my
truth without
compromise,
honoring both
my joy and
sorrow as part of
my authentic self.

• • •

I Vow to Live a Life Worth Being Known

I won't waste my breath on chasing fame,
Or playing in a surface game.
I'll let my silence guard what's true,
And let my quiet moments through.

I won't pretend to shine too bright,
I'll simply glow with steady light.
No need to shout to feel sincere,
I'll draw the ones who choose to hear.

I'll speak with heart, and act with care,
With steady hands and truths to share.
A thousand likes won't guide my way,
I'll be the one who's there to stay.

I'll grow in thought, in love, in time,
Stay grounded when the world won't rhyme.
I won't seek crowns or climb alone,
I'll lift up those who feel unknown.

So I'll strive in all I do,
To see my values carry through.
I'll forget the need to stand alone,
For I vow to live a life worth being known.

Today I will

live in a way
that reflects my
values, choosing
meaning over
attention and
depth over
display.

• • •

I Vow to Be Present in All That I Do

I vow to be present in all that I do,
To tend to each moment as if it were new.
Not rushing ahead, or clinging behind,
Meeting the now with a listening mind.

I will wake with intention, not just to begin,
To honor the breath and the life held within.
The laughter of children, the warmth of a glance,
The nearness of love when I give it a chance.

I will hear when you speak, not just with my ears,
With the stillness that quiets the weight of my fear.
No glance at the clock, no half-hearted nod,
In full-hearted presence, where silence meets God.

I will tend to each task, both routine and rare,
With steady devotion and everyday care.
For meaning is shaped not in what I pursue,
But how I attend to the work I do.

So I will meet each moment, both bitter and sweet,
With grounded attention in all that I greet.
This is the way I choose to be true:
I vow to be present in all that I do.

●

Today I will

slow down,
listen deeply,
and meet life
with my whole
heart, knowing
that presence
transforms
everything.

• • •

I Vow to Leave My Worries to the Moon

I vow to lay down all I chase,
Let night enfold me into grace.
The restless hum of thought will cease,
And in the hush, I'll welcome peace.

I will not hold what won't stay whole,
Or bend tomorrow to control.
Each hour may pass beyond my view,
Not all the world is mine to answer to.

I will make space between each breath,
Let stillness shield my joy from death.
For worry carves its lines too deep,
And steals the gentle gift of sleep.

I will return to what is true:
A quiet room, the sky's soft hue.
With loosened jaw and open chest,
I'll let my restless body rest.

So when the sun begins to rise,
I greet the day with steady eyes.
My breath moves slow, in quiet tune,
When I vow to leave my worries to the moon.

Today I will

allow myself to
pause and soften,
setting down the
weight of what
I cannot fix or
foresee. I will
trust in the quiet
of now and find
peace in simply
being.

. . .

I Vow to Belong to This Moment

I vow to loosen my old crown,
To stand unarmored, looking down.
The echoes cheer, then drift away,
I do not need them here today.

I will not chase the highest tier
Or measure worth by yesteryear.
My breath is proof I still remain,
Beyond the medals, past the strain.

I will let silence speak instead
Of who I was and what I led.
The stillness holds a different prize,
A deeper view behind the rise.

I will be present in my skin,
Not just where battles once had been.
Each step I take, unforced, unplanned,
Still honors where I choose to stand.

So when the past calls out my name
And asks I chase a fading flame,
I'll meet what's here and gently own it,
For I vow to belong to this moment.

Today I will

focus on being
grounded in
where I am,
appreciating the
value of simply
being present.

. . .

Today I will

take one honest
step forward.
I will welcome
the unknown,
honor who I am
becoming, and
trust that growth
often begins in
the dark.

. . .

Becoming Through the Break

GROWTH & TRANSFORMATION

Change is rarely gentle. It disrupts, unroots, and asks more of us than we feel ready to give. While staying the same may feel safe, it slowly withers what longs to grow. Transformation begins when we stop clinging to who we were and begin honoring who we're meant to become, even if that path is unclear.

These vows are born at the crossroads; the moments when something deep inside whispers, "Not this anymore," even before we know what comes next. Growth is not clean or quick. It is marked by missteps, restarts, and the quiet courage to keep going. These poems hold space for the slow becoming, for the pain of shedding what no longer fits and the hope of rising in a new shape.

In these verses, you'll find stories of loss that led to clarity, endings that opened the door to new beginnings, and the sacred work of coming home to yourself. They remind us that failure is not the opposite of growth; it is often the doorway. Discomfort is not a sign we are lost, but a sign we are moving.

The vows here are not about perfection. They are about movement, about honoring progress, however small, and recognizing that evolving is not a betrayal of who we were, but a deep act of alignment with who we are becoming. This chapter is a reminder that transformation is not just possible; it is necessary.

I Vow to Begin Again Without Shame

I vow to meet the morning clear,
No need to prove why I am here.
The past can stay, but not define,
It doesn't own what now is mine.

I will release what held me back,
Let go of blame, step off that track.
Each breath I take, a quiet cue
To start again and follow through.

I will not wait for perfect peace,
Or shame myself for small relief.
Instead, I'll move in honest ways,
One grounded step, not needing praise.

I will stop counting what I lack,
Or dragging all my choices back.
I'll learn from pain but not stay stuck,
My life's not built on being struck.

So when I fall, I won't pretend,
But still I'll rise and try again.
Each time I stand, I claim my name,
I vow to begin again without shame.

Today I will

honor my growth
by starting fresh
without shame,
knowing that
each step forward
is enough.

. . .

I Vow to Be the Best Version of Myself

I vow to meet myself with care,
To show up honest, soft, and bare.
Not shaped by what the world expects,
But by the love my soul reflects.

I will not trade my truth for praise,
Or blur my voice to match their ways.
I'll learn from pain I can't ignore,
And trust myself a little more.

I will be kind when I fall short,
And offer myself quiet support.
I'll breathe before I choose a word,
And honor silence when it's heard.

I will release what clouds my way,
The need to rise or prove each day.
I'll build from stillness, slow and true,
And follow what is mine to do.

So when I ache to disappear,
Or doubt my place or purpose here,
I'll rise with calm, with truth, with stealth,
I vow to be the best version of myself.

•

Today I will

pause to
acknowledge my
inner voice, let
go of the need
to perform for
approval, and
move forward
rooted in
authenticity and
grace.

• • •

I Vow to Grow Older but Never Grow Up

I vow to stay awake within,
Though time may weather my bone and skin.
The world may hurry, blur, and bend,
But I will not let my wonder end.

I will still laugh when silence falls,
And run when ocean's rhythm calls.
I'll chase the questions I once hid,
And live where wildness always did.

I will not trade my fire for rest,
Or hush the dreams within my chest.
Though seasons pull with quiet tide,
I'll meet each ending clear and wide.

I will accept what age imparts,
But guard the light within my heart.
Though life is measured by strict design,
I'll keep a space for the divine.

So when the world says, "Settle down,"
I'll smile and dance beyond their frown.
For joy is mine to fill my cup,
I vow to grow older but never grow up.

•

Today I will

remember that
age does not
define my joy,
and I will honor
the youthful light
within me no
matter what the
world expects.

• • •

I Vow to Stay Strong Today and Be Stronger Tomorrow

I vow to stand, though winds may sway,
To meet what comes and not give way.
I will plant my feet in shifting ground
And root myself where strength is found.

I will rise today with aching hands
And carry on with what life demands.
The world may press from every side;
Still, I will hold my peace inside.

When doubt arrives, it speaks with weight
Of all I missed and learned too late.
I will pause, breathe deep, and let it speak;
But I will not let it make me weak.

I will lean into the work I bear,
The quiet strength that keeps me there.
Each step will be a thread I weave
In who I am and what I believe.

So I vow this, in calm and sorrow:
To stay strong today, be stronger tomorrow.
Not for applause, proof, or pride,
But to stand for who I am inside.

Today I will

stand rooted in
who I am, even
when life feels
uncertain. I will
listen to doubt
without letting
it define me, and
trust that each
step I take today
prepares me for
greater strength
tomorrow.

• • •

I Vow Never to Settle for Less Than I Deserve

I vow to seek what stirs my soul,
Not simply fill a hollow hole.
I will not stay where love is thin,
Or call a half-lived life a win.

I will not trade my dreams for rest,
Or hush my voice to please the rest.
I will trust the slow and daring climb,
And keep the quiet of my time.

I will not wear a borrowed name,
Or walk a path that dulls my flame.
I will find work that makes me rise,
Not just grow small beneath the skies.

I will not barter joy for peace,
Or let my truest hungers cease.
I will ask more of every day,
And listen when my heart would say.

So, when still waters call me near,
I'll step beyond what soothes my fear.
I'll shape a life I know I serve,
And vow never to settle for less than I deserve.

Today I will

choose boldly,
trust my inner
voice, and hold
my life to the
highest standard
of my soul's true
worth.

• • •

I Vow to Rise with Every Fall

I vow to rise when I am down,
To meet the dust, then leave the ground,
Not with a shout, but quiet will,
The kind that holds me steady still.

I will mask the weight I bear
And smile to hide the ache that's there.
I'll name the truth, then let it stay,
And meet myself in full each day.

I will not run from my missteps,
But learn the shape of each regret.
I'll trace the thread within the mess
And mend it into gentleness.

I will return when strength feels thin,
Begin again from deep within.
Though slow at times, I'll choose to move
And let my living be my proof.

So when the night feels cold and wide,
And shadows press from every side,
I'll breathe, stand up, and face it all.
I vow to rise with every fall.

Today I will

embrace my
imperfections
as part of my
becoming.
I will meet
myself where I
am, honor my
process, and
choose to rise
again, gently,
purposefully, and
with grace.

. . .

I Vow to Find My Purpose

I vow to bring my full self into play,
Not just show up, but give my soul away.
Not to be drained, but to feel more alive,
To do the kind of work where I can thrive.

I will put heart into the things I make,
Let meaning grow with every risk I take.
I'll stay aware of what lights me inside,
And follow where my curiosity guides.

I will create from truth, not just for show,
Let passion shape the rhythm of my flow.
Whether it's quiet or boldly expressed,
I'll give each piece of me my honest best.

I will stay open, even when it's hard,
Keep choosing depth instead of playing guard.
My purpose isn't something I should chase,
It's what I build when I hold my own space.

So when I question where or why I start,
I'll check back in with what still moves my heart.
Each step, a thread that pulls me unrehearsed,
I vow to find my purpose.

Today I will

show up
wholeheartedly,
stay curious,
and create from
a place of truth,
trusting that
my purpose is
revealed through
how I live each
moment.

. . .

I Vow Death Will Find Me Fierce and Alive

I vow when death arrives with silent grace,
Light will still shine upon my face.
Passion will blaze in my heart and mind,
No trace of life will be left behind.

I vow each step I take be bold and true,
With dreams pursued and purpose too.
Let laughter echo, rich and wide,
No path untaken, none denied.

Though time may steal my years away,
It shall not break or halt my stay.
I will greet the dawn, embrace the night,
And dance until the stars ignite.

For life is not just breath and bone,
But fire and love through me has grown.
To truly live is to ignite,
And leave the world still bathed in light.

So when death knocks, let it see,
My soul has burned untamed and free.
For it may take, but can't deprive,
I vow death will find me fierce and alive.

•

Today I will

live with fearless
intent, choosing
boldness over
hesitation, and
making each
moment count as
part of my legacy.

• • •

I Vow to Dance Until the Stars Ignite

I vow to dance, though silence falls,
Though night drapes thick along the walls.
When joy feels far and light runs thin,
I'll let the music rise within.

I will not wait for skies to clear,
But move through doubt and breathe through fear.
Each step a truth I choose to trust,
Each turn a letting go of dust.

I will not dance for eyes to see,
But for the fire that moves in me,
A quiet blaze, a steady thread,
A way to speak what stays unsaid.

I will stay near when hope is slight,
And draw from stillness what feels right.
Even in silence, I remain,
A body singing through the strain.

So when the hush outlasts the flame,
And nothing near me feels the same,
I will move forward through the night.
I vow to dance until the stars ignite.

Today I will

honor my inner
light and move
with intention,
even when the
world feels dim.
I will trust in my
quiet strength
and let my truth
be expressed
through my
actions, regardless
of who is
watching or what
lies ahead.

. . .

•

Today I will

will listen
with empathy,
respond with
kindness, and
offer grace
instead of
judgment. I
will choose
connection, even
when it feels
easier to turn
away.

• • •

Bridges Built in Silence

CONNECTION & COMPASSION

Connection is not always found in conversation. Sometimes it lives in shared stillness, in the comfort of simply being with someone without needing to explain. We often think love must be loud, full of words, gestures, and constant affirmation. But true compassion is quieter. It listens more than it speaks. It stays even when there's nothing to say.

There is something sacred in the quiet between people; a presence that asks nothing but offers everything. These are the moments when we hold space for someone else's truth without interrupting it with our own. Connection deepens when we stop trying to fix and instead choose just to be there.

The poems in this chapter honor the people who stayed and offered quiet understanding instead of solutions. They speak to the kind of love that doesn't push or pull but remains steady. These verses remember the power of a hand-held, a pause respected, a truth heard without judgment, and remind us to offer that same quiet understanding when it's our turn to stay.

The vows here are rooted in gentleness. They call us to be a safe place for others and for ourselves, to lead with kindness rather than certainty, and to reach across the quiet not to fill it but to share it. Connection is not always found in words; it's often built in presence, one steady moment at a time.

I Vow to Be Happy in My Own Skin

I vow to rest where I begin,
To meet my breath and settle in.
No mask to wear, no part to play,
Just me, unshaped by what they say.

I will not trade my shape for grace,
Or shrink to fit another's space.
I'll name the shame that lived too near,
And meet it now without the fear.

I will not flinch at mirrors' gaze,
Or chase the shine of younger days.
Each freckle, line, or softened place
Will mark the storms I chose to face.

I will speak kind when doubt takes hold,
And keep my word when I've been bold.
I'll listen close to what I need,
And let compassion take the lead.

So, when the rush of life feels tight,
And shadows stretch beyond the light,
Whatever shape my days begin,
I vow to be happy in my own skin.

Today I will

honor who I
am becoming,
embracing every
part of myself
as worthy and
whole.

• • •

I Vow to Be a Kid Again

I vow to meet the world with play,
To loosen all I gripped today.
To let my thoughts be wide and bright,
Unburdened by the need for right.

I will remember how to share,
Even when life feels less than fair.
I'll name my needs without disguise,
And meet hard truths with steady eyes.

I will stay curious, not cold,
Ask why, and listen as I'm told.
I'll praise the odd, embrace the new,
And let small wonders shape my view.

I will forgive the way kids do,
Quick to mend and start new.
I won't keep score or hold what's past;
Not every hurt is meant to last.

So when the world grows sharp and thin,
I'll breathe, and let the play begin.
I'll remember joy that lived back when,
I vow to be a kid again.

Today I will

meet life with
childlike joy,
forgive quickly,
and delight in
simple wonders.

. . .

I Vow to Leave Footprints of Kindness Wherever I Go

I vow to walk through life with open hands,
To soften ground where each foot lands.
The world may press with speed and strain,
But I will take the slower lane.

I will speak with care when words feel sharp,
And lend my silence where griefs embark.
Small acts, unnoticed, I will give,
To show the quiet way to live.

I will not wait for skies to clear,
To be the warmth when storms draw near.
A door held wide, a name recalled,
These things, though simple, are not small at all.

I will forgive, though pride resists,
And meet cold shoulders with loosened fists.
The gift of grace I've long received,
I'll pass along, though not perceived.

So when the day has met its end,
I'll count each stranger as a friend.
One quiet step can help hope flow,
I vow to leave footprints of kindness wherever I go.

•

Today I will

choose kindness
in small ways,
remembering
that each
thoughtful
action can ripple
outward and
leave lasting
impressions of
warmth and hope
in others' lives.

• • •

I Vow to Be a Story in Someone's Life

I vow to leave a page behind,
Not in the grand, but in the kind.
A thread of warmth in someone's day,
A voice that helps them find their way.

I will not wait for roles to shine,
But speak when silence feels like mine.
I'll hold a gaze, I'll learn a name,
And stay when others shift to blame.

I will be steady, close, and near,
A shelter when the winds grow clear.
My presence won't be loud or bold,
But something true they gently hold.

I'll ask the questions few have asked,
And listen long, not rush them past.
I'll carry parts they give to me,
And guard them with humility.

So when they speak of love that stays,
Of quiet hands that shaped their days,
They'll say I moved with gentle life,
I vow to be a story in someone's life.

Today I will

be a steady,
caring presence
in someone's life,
offering patience,
empathy, and
gentle support
without seeking
recognition.

• • •

I Vow No Soul Will Stand Alone Today

I vow to stand for those betrayed and lost,
Who bear the weight, who count the cost.
The beaten down, the ones who fall,
I'll lift them up, I'll heed their call.

I will hear the quiet cries they hide,
The weary truth they hold inside.
Though words may fail or drift away,
I'll stay to face when others stray.

I will hold fast when hope is thin,
A light unshaken from within.
For even stone can break and wear
Without a soul who stops to care.

I will believe in who they are,
Their unseen wounds, each hidden scar.
And through the dark, I'll walk beside,
Not to fix, but to provide.

So I will guard, I will remain,
A shelter strong through loss and strain.
Though others turn and walk away,
I vow no soul will stand alone today.

●

Today I will

choose to be a
steadfast source
of comfort
and solidarity
for those who
feel unseen or
abandoned.

• • •

I Vow to Love Like It's My Job

I vow to rise with heart in hand,
To meet the day, to understand.
Not waiting on the world to prove,
I will show up daily, steady and true.

I will not count what love returns,
And let regret become what burns.
I'll ask with grace, I'll stay with care,
Even when silence fills the air.

I will forgive without a cue,
In what I say and what I do.
I'll give with hands that need no claim,
And carry kindness without name.

I will not rush to be repaid,
Or weigh the cost of love conveyed.
My presence will be soft but strong,
Even when the days feel long.

So when the weight is hard to bear,
And no one sees the way I care,
I'll take a breath, reset, and nod,
Then love again, like it's my job.

Today I will

offer love freely
and consistently,
making kindness
a responsibility
rather than a
reward.

• • •

I Vow to Know Love

I vow to seek love in all that I do,
In whispers of dawn and the night's gentle hue.
Through trials that threaten to darken my way,
I'll cherish its warmth and bid it to stay.

No tempest shall silence the kindness I weave,
For love is the breath in the life that I lead.
In sorrow, in joy, through moments so bright,
I'll hold onto love with all of my might.

Not just in passion that flickers and wanes,
But deep in the roots where devotion remains.
In friendships that heal, in hands that console,
In quiet embraces that strengthen the soul.

For love is a vow both steady and true,
A beacon of light when the world feels undue.
It asks for no gold, no fortune, no prize,
Just hearts that are open and free of disguise.

So, I vow to know love in all that I see,
In kindness, in truth, in all given to me.
No matter how distant, how trying the road,
I'll carry its weight as my heart's sacred code.

Today I will

open my heart to
give and receive
love in its many
forms. I will look
for love in the
small gestures,
speak from
compassion, and
let connection
guide my actions.

. . .

I Vow to Find Love Again

I vow to let the silence stay,
To sit with all that slipped away.
No need to chase what wasn't mine,
Or beg the past to send a sign.

I will take time to learn my name,
And free myself from ghost and blame.
I'll walk through days both wide and slow,
And trust there's more I've yet to know.

I will return to quiet joy with grace,
And meet my life in every place.
I'll cook, I'll sing, I'll speak, I'll try,
And walk the earth with a seeing eye.

I will not ache for what they find,
A softer voice, a gentler mind.
I'll let them go, release the pain,
And face the sun through wind and rain.

So I'll meet the world with open skin,
Let warmth and breath return within.
I will walk with trust that time will mend,
For I vow to find love again.

·

Today I will

honor the love
I carry within
and welcome the
future with hope
and readiness.

·   ·   ·

I Vow to Carry You in Breath and Tone

I vow to carry you in breath and tone,
In spaces soft and mine alone,
Not carved in stone or marked by flame,
But held where silence speaks your name.

I will recall you without speech,
In moments memory longs to reach,
A hush that rises through my chest,
And tells of you when words must rest.

I will not chase what time has taken,
Or fold into the ache, forsaken.
I'll move with you through all I do,
A part of me, still shaped by you.

I will not bend beneath the weight,
But shape it into what I create:
A sigh, a song, a whispered name
That brings your light through loss and pain.

So when the hush of night is near,
And all that's left is what I hear,
I'll close my eyes and feel you home,
I vow to carry you in breath and tone.

•

Today I will

honor the
memory of
those I've lost by
allowing love to
move through
me, quietly,
creatively, and
without sorrow's
weight.

• • •

•

Today I will

notice what
remains, not
what is missing.
I'll welcome
quiet blessings,
offer myself
grace, and let
enough be
enough.

• • •

The Light That Was Always There

Always There

GRATITUDE & GRACE

Gratitude is the practice of noticing what's good and holding it close. It's about being thankful, not just for the big moments but for the small ones we often overlook. A warm conversation. A quiet morning. A breath that comes easier than the last. When we slow down enough to notice these things, we start to see how much is still right in front of us.

Grace works in much the same way. It doesn't need to be earned or explained. It meets us where we are and reminds us we're allowed to begin again. Even on hard days, there's something soft to hold onto, a kind gesture, a bit of beauty, a moment of peace. These aren't loud or showy, but they stay with us. They remind us that we're not alone.

The poems in this chapter reflect on what remains when the noise fades: the people who stood by us, the kindness that asked for nothing, the small joys that helped us through. They remind us to say thank you more often, not just out loud, but with how we move through the world.

The vows here encourage us to see clearly, receive freely, and carry appreciation into each day. Gratitude is not about pretending everything is perfect; it's about choosing to notice what's still good. And grace is knowing we're still worthy of joy, even in the midst of struggle. Both are reminders that the light was never gone. It was just waiting to be seen.

I Vow to Choose Grace Over Grudges

I vow to pause before I speak,
To steady thoughts when they turn bleak.
When rooms grow tense and tempers rise,
I will meet the moment with clearer eyes.

I will not let a glance offend,
Or make a stranger my loose end.
If someone sighs or forgets to care,
I will grant them breath and leave it there.

I will not cling to what is mine,
A seat, a space, some perfect line.
If another lingers, unaware,
I will step aside and choose to share.

I will not trade my calm for blame,
Or keep a fire that has no aim.
If holding anger burns too long,
I will choose a way that keeps me strong.

So when the world feels heavy with edges,
And every slight deepens old ledges,
I will soften my heart where mercy judges,
And vow to choose grace over grudges.

·

Today I will

pause and
respond with
grace, releasing
the need to be
right or offended.

· · ·

I Vow to Live in the Now

I vow to walk with quiet grace,
And meet each moment face to face.
To feel the ground beneath my feet,
And honor quiet when we meet.

I will not take this life for granted,
Each moment rare, each moment planted.
The warmth of sun, a quiet breeze,
I'll carry them all with gentle ease.

I will forgive and not hold tight
To every wrong or need to fight.
I'll let go first, release the weight,
And clear a softer path from hate.

I will love fully, heart and mind,
With nothing held and all aligned.
I'll show my care through what I do,
And let my actions speak what's true.

So as I live the vows I make,
To love, forgive, stay wide awake,
When my life takes its final bow,
I can rest, knowing I lived in the now.

•

Today I will

slow down,
notice the gifts
around me, and
act with love and
awareness. I will
live each moment
as a chance to
be grounded,
grateful, and
true.

• • •

I Vow to Count Moments, Not Things

I vow to stop mistaking more for full,
To loosen life from keeping score or pull.
To stop the chase that never ends,
And learn what truly fills, not bends.

I will count the light at break of day,
The way a friend's laugh bends my way.
The hush before the coffee brews,
The smile I wear at welcome news.

I will count the joy when someone wins,
The warmth that rises from within.
The talks that drift and never end,
The kind that say: I'm here, my friend.

I will notice how the sunset leans,
The beauty tucked in in-between.
The start of days that softly rise,
Without a need to monetize.

So when I look back on my days,
Not weighed by worth or outer praise,
I'll see all the joys that life still brings,
I vow to count moments, not things.

Today I will

pause to notice
what fills my
heart, not my
shelves.

. . .

I Vow to Expect Nothing but Appreciate Everything

I vow to walk without a list in hand,
No hidden hopes, no strict demand.
What comes, comes freely,unreserved,
Not something I feel I've deserved.

I will give with no return in mind,
Let every act be warm and kind.
If grace flows back, I will receive,
But I give not hoping to achieve.

I will notice joy in all that's near,
A simple meal, a voice sincere.
When life leans in with something sweet,
I'll bow in thanks and feel complete.

I will not wait with arms outstretched,
Or mark my worth by what's been fetched.
But when love shows, in any form,
I'll hold it close and keep it warm.

So I will live with hands unclosed,
With quiet hope, not goals imposed.
And when life gives, my heart will sing:
I vow to expect nothing but appreciate everything.

●

Today I will

surrender my
need for control
and outcomes,
choosing instead
to notice and
cherish life's quiet
offerings with a
grateful spirit.

• • •

I Vow to Find Joy Without Conditions

I vow to stop waiting for life to align,
To stop holding back until things feel fine.
Joy isn't earned when the chaos is gone,
It shows up in coffee, in walking at dawn.

I will learn to notice what's already there,
A deep breath, a moment, the scent in the air.
I won't let the hard days define what I see,
I'll find quiet places that steady me.

I will let laughter come loose in my chest,
And stop tying joy to the size of success.
I won't chase more just to feel at peace,
I'll trust in enough and let striving cease.

I will not wait for the noise to be still,
To sing with the birds or walk up the hill.
I'll count what is simple as more than it seems,
A full glass of water, a pocket of dreams.

So when the day doesn't offer delight,
I'll still find joy in the edges of night.
Not because everything's met my ambitions,
But because I vow to find joy without conditions.

Today I will

choose joy even
when things feel
incomplete

. . .

I Vow to Be Grateful for Everything I Have in My Life

I vow to meet each morning with open eyes,
To trace the quiet blessings that never disguise.
Even the simplest breath, the warmth of light,
Carries a grace too vast for sight.

I will not wait for comfort to appear,
But name what's good when it draws near.
A hand to hold, a steady floor,
These are the riches I'll ask no more.

I will pause in moments others might miss,
And let small mercies rise like mist.
Not every joy comes dressed in gold,
Some whisper truths that make me bold.

I will not chase what I do not need,
Or let comparison plant a seed.
Instead, I'll tend the life I grow,
And find enough in what I know.

So when the noise begins to press,
I'll turn toward quiet thankfulness.
My heart will live in peace with what feels right,
I vow to be grateful for everything I have in my life.

•

Today I will

slow down,
notice the gifts
already in my
life, and let
gratitude shape
my heart.

• • •

I Vow to Carry Grace in All I Do

I vow to wait when I feel rushed,
to hold my ground when I've been crushed.
Not every moment needs my say,
I'll let some storms just pass their way.

I will choose mercy when I'm burned,
release the need to get returned.
No quiet score will guide my hand,
I'll free the weight I used to plan.

I will stay humble when I win,
not feed the urge to rise within.
When pride invites me to be more,
I'll listen first before I roar.

I will find peace when things go wide,
when plans collapse or rules collide.
I won't let noise decide my path,
I'll move beneath the weight of wrath.

So when reaction calls my name,
and I could strike to shield my shame,
I'll lean on love that pulls me through,
I vow to carry grace in all I do.

Today I will

slow down,
reflect before I
act, and allow
grace to guide
me through
moments of
challenge and
pride alike.

. . .

Continuing the Conversation

Thank you for sharing your time and spirit with these poems. If you'd like to stay connected and keep exploring, I invite you to join me beyond these pages.

Scan the QR code below or visit https://thirdcrown.news/Conversation to access additional poems, behind-the-scenes reflections, audio readings, and a private space created just for readers. This is a place for honest conversation, new perspectives, and deeper connection.

I hope to meet you there.

With gratitude,

-Vanelli